An Instant Playscri

ROAD MOVIE

Godfrey Hamilton

NICK HERN
BOOKS
London

in association with

CHAPMAN DUNCAN
PRODUCTIONS
London

Road Movie was first performed at the Tron Theatre, Glasgow, on 1 August 1995, before transferring to the Traverse Theatre, Edinburgh, on 22 August for the 1995 Edinburgh Festival. In the original Starving Artists' production all the roles were played by

MARK PINKOSH

Director: Lorenzo Mele
Lighting: Douglas Kuhrt

An Instant Playscript

Road Movie first published in Great Britain in l996 as a paperback original by Nick Hern Books Ltd, 14 Larden Road, London W3 7ST in association with Chapman Duncan Productions, London.

Road Movie copyright © 1995 Godfrey I. Hamilton

Godfrey Hamilton has asserted his right to be identified as the author of this work

Typeset by the author
Re-formatted to publisher's specification by Country Setting, Woodchurch, Kent TN26 3TB
Printed and bound in Great Britain

ISBN 1 85459 301 3

A CIP catalogue record for this book is available from the British Library

Chapman Duncan Productions Ltd
presents
Starving Artists
in

ROAD MOVIE

**by Godfrey Hamilton
Performed by Mark Pinkosh
Directed by Lorenzo Mele
Lighting Designed by Douglas Kuhrt
Stage Managed by Jessica Moore**

General Management by Sebastian Warrack for Chapman Duncan Associates.
Press and Marketing by Chapman Duncan Associates .
Leaflet and poster design by Sightlines.

The producers would like to thank: Simon Lawson of Dillons Arts Bookshop, Everyone at the Lyric Theatre Hammersmith, Darren Wood at First Call, Julie Parker, Francis Alexander

MARK PINKOSH (Performer) and **GODFREY HAMILTON** (Writer)

American Mark Pinkosh and Londoner Godfrey Hamilton are Starving Artists Theatre Company. The Company was founded in 1983, and for its first ten years was based in Honolulu, Hawaii. Until early 1993, when they relocated to California, Mark and Godfrey's theatre was the only company in the State of Hawaii presenting alternative and fringe theatre.

In 1992 Mark and Godfrey were honoured, in a public ceremony, by the City and County of Honolulu for their work counteracting homophobia and racism in Hawaii.

'Gaining an ever-stronger reputation on both sides of the Atlantic' (London Evening Standard), Mark won the Stage Award for Best Actor at the 1995 Edinburgh Festival. Godfrey's plays have been seen all over Britain and played extensive seasons in London: *Kissing Marianne* (1994) was commissioned by the Drill Hall, London, and has just been published in the anthology *Staging Gay Lives* (Westview/Harper Collins).

Mark and Godfrey's previous work together includes *Island to Island* (1988), *Angles of Freedom* (1990), a radical re-working of *Peer Gynt* (1991), *Holding Back the Ocean* (1991). *Broken Folk* (1992), *Haole Boy* (1992) and *To Men in Love* (1993).

Sleeping with You premiered at the 1993 Edinburgh Festival (Traverse Theatre, Edinburgh), transferred to BAC's main house for a season, and subsequently toured to New Zealand where it headlined at Auckland's Hero Festival of Lesbian and Gay Arts. The show then played seasons in Los Angeles (twice), Honolulu, Calgary and San Francisco, having earned nominations for the Independent Theatre Award and London Fringe Awards.

Road Movie won a Fringe First Award at the 1995 Edinburgh Festival (Traverse Theatre, Edinburgh), and recently played at the Toronto du Maurier World Stage Festival. This year Starving Artists will premiere their new play *Viper's Opium* at the Traverse Theatre.

Starving Artists can be contacted at 4377 1/2 Camero Avenue, Los Angeles CA 90027 or c/o Chapman Duncan Associates, 10 -14 Macklin Street, London WC2B 5NF

LORENZO MELE (Director)

Recent work includes *Viper's Opium*, Starving Artists' 1996 Edinburgh Fetival production, and *Molly's Collar*, a devised piece based on hidden lesbian and gay histories in Scotland. Previous work includes a Strathclyde schools tour of Shakespeare's *Romeo and Juliet*, in a new adaption by John Clifford, for RSAMD; *The Cub* by Stephanie McKnight

for the Traverse Theatre Edinburgh; *Forbidden Pleasures* by Alasdair Cameron at the Citizens Theatre Glasgow. He has devised and performed work with Singaporean Theatre Company: The Necessary Stage. Other directorial work has included a young people's performance commissioned by Children First, *Medea*, *The Children's Hour*, and *Bent*.

DOUGLAS KUHRT
(Lighting Designer)

Douglas trained at Croydon College and was resident at the Warehouse Theatre Croydon where he lit more than 20 productions, including *The Fishing Trip* (directed by Lindsay Anderson) and *Playing Sinatra* (also at Greenwich). Other work includes *Fascinating Aida* (Lyric Hammersmith and tour) *Cavalcade* (Churchill, Bromley and tour), *The Night Larry Kramer Kissed Me* , *Kissing Marianne* and *Road Movie* (Traverse, Edinburgh), *The Fabulous Lypsinka Show* (Drill Hall), *Sweet Phoebe* (Sydney Theatre Company), *Temporary Girl* (Cockpit), *Jimeoin* (Cochrane), *Over Hear* (Bristol Old Vic), *Kiss of the Spider Woman* (Leicester Haymarket) and *Definitely Doris* (Kings Head).

Previous work for Starving Artists includes *Kissing Marianne* (Drill Hall and Traverse, Edinburgh) and *Road Movie* (Traverse, Edinburgh and Toronto Festival),

JESSICA MOORE
(Stage Manager)

Since leaving LAMDA three years ago Jess has worked on various shows for the Citizens Theatre, Glasgow, Theatr Clwyd, Mold, Hampstead Theatre and *Indian Ink* at the Aldwych Theatre.

Chapman Duncan Associates/Chapman Duncan Productions Ltd

Guy Chapman set up Chapman Duncan Associates, a press and marketing agency, in 1994; and Chapman Duncan Productions Ltd in 1995; both with Cameron Duncan. Productions include for CDA: Phyllis Nagy's award-winning *Disappeared* (co-produced with Leicester Haymarket and Midnight Theatre Company – tour and Royal Court Theatre) and for CDP: Andrew Alty's *Something About Us* (Lyric Theatre Hammersmith). Also Jimmy Murphy's *Brothers of the Brush* (co-production between Guy Chapman, William Butler-Sloss and Soho Theatre Company at the Arts Theatre).

For Chapman Duncan Productions Ltd

Directors: Guy Chapman, Cameron Duncan, Andrew Toole

For Chapman Duncan Associates

Guy Chapman
Steven Drew
Andrew Toole
Sebastian Warrack
Yan Foo

10-14 Macklin Street, London WC2B 5NF (0171 242 1882)

Characters

JOEL	Early 30's. East Coast.
SCOTT	Early 30's. California.
MA DEVA	Mid 50's. Southern Belle.
MYRA	Maybe 50's, maybe 60's. Arizona.
DHARMA	Late 20's, California New Age.

The text is for Mark, with love.

1. A vast desert highway. Sundown.
Joel stands by his car. He is in his early thirties,
handsome, dishevelled, a day or two's stubble;
a man who has driven a long way without much sleep.

JOEL: Around six-fifteen / in the evening
the sky turns vast lilac and green
and the mountains turn purple, indigo,
and then some colors I never saw before
and some colors I never heard of
and the highway goes on forever.
The radio is full of desert rock and roll,
dry twangy sounds like lizards scuttling underneath
rocks and things / peeking out from under tumbleweed.
   And
a wind blows off the desert and it *does* roll,
   tumbleweed,
gently across the highway and
I turn the radio off and
I'm on a big, dark, darkening indigo and purple plain,
a desert, reaching off to the horizon, to slide under
   those
craggy deep purple mountains.
And because there are little songs about everything
I sing *Deep Purple*
under my breath:
'When the deep purple falls -'
then louder,
'- over sleepy garden walls'
because I realize I'm scared.

2. New York City. Expressway. Late afternoon rush hour.

JOEL: Smile.
Smile damn you !
Have a nice day have a good evening have a nice life
have a *nice* day. 'Jesus loves you'
'Honk if you love Jesus'
'honk if you're horny' -
bumper sticker life fuckin' bumper sticker world.

'God said it / I believe it / That settles it'
'Piss off a liberal - buy a gun'
'Your car is your portable psychic space. Make it your
      own !'
Nice turn, mister ! O, go blow it out your ass !
I'm only gonna smile at people I like !

No more grinning at the bagger in Safeway, at the
      checkout -
'Paper or plastic ?'
I DON'T FUCKING KNOW YOU TELL ME.
Have a nice day.
Why ?

It's a personalized number plate life.
I LUV U 2. NUTS 4U. BIG IN L A.
Visualize world peace.
Hey, visualize your ass in a sling.
Visualize my dick in your ear !
I'm a good kind person.
I'm nice to animals and small children.
I pay my taxes. I'm a *good citizen.*
So why don't I have nice suits ? Huh ?
I want nice suits. Yeah.
I wanna suits that cost ... Oprah money.
I want David Letterman familiarity, y'know ?
I wanna go in pizza places in New York City,
have people recognize me. 'HEY JOEL HOW YA
      DOIN' !
LOVED YA SHOW LAST NIGHT !'

I smiled at her everyday. I don't even know her name.
The woman in the parking garage
the woman who checks your ticket takes your money.
Lets you out.

I said:
how are you today ?
Her curled lip, snarling, under her breath
'Yeah right. Like you care'.

Hey. Hey, I'm sorry that you're in a little wooden box
inside a parking structure inside a solid city,
I'm sorry you're breathing gas all day, but hey, I said
'Have a nice day'. Now why did she do that ?
That's all it takes.
'Like you care.'

I don't. I should thank her for that.
I've spent the bigger part of my life
pretending I care.

Neighbors whose name I don't know or want to know.
Kids who're scared of me. Dogs that growl at my
    offered hand.
Friends whose only recommendation is familiarity.
Needing the safety of my history with them,
the easiness of our little social shorthands.
That's not friendship, is it ?
That's not the touch in the dark that stops the terrors.
That's not his breath on my eyelids that lulls me to
    sleep.
That's not, is it, is it ?
You were right, Scott.
It just took one person: 'Like you care'.
It set me off, riding, in my car. I'm coming Scott.
I'm coming for you, you and the ocean.
I can smell it already.
Ocean. 2 billion years -

HEY ! PICK A LANE MISTER ! ANY LANE ! HEY !
HEY ! AND UP YOURS TOO !

Hey Scott ! Hey !
Listen ! You were right !
I did it ! I did it !
I'm doing it !

What a long way from sliding down walls
looking for that little piece of me -

3. Gay bar. Lights & music.

JOEL: Looking for that little piece of me,
               to see myself reflected in his eyes
               Looking for that tiny broken piece of me
               through the barriers of the night.
               Dark damp places / cold shadowed places / dry places
               among rocks. Heavy places in the corners of the night
               under the cold freeways / smoke and bars / here's
               the man of my dreams
               clutching a can o' beer and
               a handful of speed / vein full of dark powder but
               hey, hey, he's got bricks for a belly
               thick neck big tits that's the man for me -
               take me
               take me back to the bars
               take me back to the barriers and walls of the night -

hey mister d'you have it ?
I'm missing a piece of me.
In here, something got ... I lost it,
I don't know where
or how ... I dropped it on a beach a street a field
I'm sorry I'm sorry please please help me find it ...

hey you / d'you got it ? / It. I want it I need it. It.
The bit of my gut that feels.
The place in my heart that encloses him.
The secret me. My demon lover my dream lover
my guardian angel -
hey man are you him ? Are you the one I need ?
Take me / touch me
JUST TOUCH ME LIKE YOU MEAN IT
just touch me like I don't disgust you.
I'll do whatever you want, just touch me please,
need me / please / please want me as much as I want
     you
I'm lookin' in the alleyways
I'm runnin' down these slick wet streets -
hey man are you the one who'll need me the rest of my
     life ?
Wow o wow. I'm lookin' in some very strange places
for the love of my life.
I swear I heard him / smelled him / felt his breath
before I knew what such things mean.

4.   *Sausalito, near San Francisco. A houseboat. Night.*
     Moonlight through windows. Scott is staring at Joel.
     Scott is slightly younger; energetic, attractive, with dazzling eyes.

JOEL: Oh .... God almighty .... hi.

SCOTT: Hi.

JOEL: Hi.

SCOTT: Hi.

JOEL: Do I know you ?

SCOTT: Not as well as I know you.

JOEL: What happened ?

SCOTT: Your liver had enough.

JOEL:	How'd I get here ? Where is here ?
SCOTT:	I'm your Good Samaritan. Do you do this often ?
JOEL:	What ?
SCOTT:	Get loaded.
JOEL:	No ! No. Someone poisoned my highball. Someone with a grudge. Who knew ?
SCOTT:	You're much prettier when you're sober.
JOEL:	And you would be ... ?
SCOTT:	Scott.
JOEL:	Scott. How ...
SCOTT:	Adventurous. Like Scott of the Antartic.
JOEL:	Well. Right now I feel like a low rent Captain Oates.
SCOTT:	You were lying in the gutter.
JOEL:	Thank you.
SCOTT:	Facedown.
JOEL:	Thank you. And you what ... you introduced yourself ?
SCOTT:	You drink too much.
JOEL:	So ?
SCOTT:	It will kill you.
JOEL:	And your point would be ?
SCOTT:	You deserve better. It's a tacky way to die.
JOEL:	Not very glam, no.
SCOTT:	Ugly. sleazy.
JOEL:	Not romantic ?
SCOTT:	Not romantic, no. Staying alive is a much more interesting choice.
JOEL:	It is ?

SCOTT:	It is. You just haven't realized it yet.
JOEL:	Well excuse me, Scott, I've beeen trying to - look, just who the fuck are you because frankly this is starting to scare me -
SCOTT:	I'm Scott. I was at the press reception. You ... um... I think the expression is 'struck up' a conversation ... sort of ... it was a bit one-sided.
JOEL:	Oh God. What did we discuss ?
SCOTT:	You discussed.
JOEL:	Me, what did me discuss. *I* discuss ?
SCOTT:	Um. Andy Warhol. Lou Reed. Tarkovsky. Not necessarily in that order. You certainly have a lot of ... opinions.
JOEL:	Oh. Was I angry ?
SCOTT:	Furious. People don't listen to you much, do they ?
JOEL:	Excuse *me* I -
SCOTT:	You wanted someone to listen. You sounded lonely.
JOEL:	Why are you doing this ?
SCOTT:	So I can feel sanctimonious.
JOEL:	You do it well.
SCOTT:	And self righteous.
JOEL:	Just don't tell me I should smile more often.
SCOTT:	Smile ? What for ?
JOEL:	Just don't, is all. OK ? And once more: where am I ?
SCOTT:	My place.
JOEL:	Which is where ?
SCOTT:	Sausalito.
JOEL:	Sausalito - a houseboat ?!

SCOTT:	It won't drift away.
JOEL:	A houseboat ! Puffpuff ! Are you wealthy?
SCOTT:	No.
JOEL:	Oh. Are you a freeloader ?
SCOTT:	Nope.
JOEL:	Oh. Sausalito !
SCOTT:	It's temporary. I move around a lot.
JOEL:	It's someone else's home. Isn't it. Don't lie to me ! We broke in to someone else's home.
SCOTT:	No. We didn't.
JOEL:	Look, can I go now?
SCOTT:	Where ?
JOEL:	What day is it ? Is it Sunday yet ?
SCOTT:	It's Monday. Morning.
JOEL:	Monday ! Jeezis I have a plane to catch ! OWWW! My *head !*
SCOTT:	No you don't. Just this once. It can wait.
JOEL:	You don't understand. I have to get back to New York.
SCOTT:	Do you ? Do you ?
JOEL:	What. *What ?*
SCOTT:	Stay awhile. You can puke all you want. All you need. I have plastic buckets. See? You already filled the purple one.
JOEL:	O man. I'm losing my touch. Time was I could handle these press junkets. I was at a reception once, I passed out, clutching my drink, I slid down the wall, I didn't spill a drop. I came to, they said I'd been out about an hour. I took a big gulp and - 'Where're these godammed celebrities I'm supposed to be pitching ?' Someone said 'Rosie Perez was

13

stepping over you all evening' - Dad taught me to
drink like a gentleman.

SCOTT: You represent Rosie Perez ?

JOEL: Did I say that ? 'Don't murder good whisky with soda
           and ice   - that's ADULTERY !' My Dad taught
           me that.

SCOTT: Um ... is that all he taught you ?

JOEL: Pretty much, yeah.

SCOTT: I'll get you some water. You're very dehydrated.

JOEL: OK I get it. You're from one of those funny meetings
           aren't you. All God and twelve steps and don't
           drink just for today and whoopee I learned to
           change a light bulb -

SCOTT: No. No I'm not. And what if I am ?

JOEL: What if you are. Oh God. Hey. Hey, Scott ... did you
           ...did you do anything ? While I was passed out ?

SCOTT: You weren't passed out. You were very lively. And no.
           No. I didn't. You weren't very tasty.

JOEL: Ogod I can't see. O my head hurts. My teeth ache.
           Oh. Dear. Scott. Scott.

SCOTT: Whaddya need ?

JOEL: A bucket. Do you have a pink one ?

           He touches my forehead, I feel safe and calm.
           On his wrist, a silver band. Strong, flexible. A silver
           band bent round his wrist. Like a lizard curled
           around the bone. A name stamped into it.

JOEL: So ... who's that ?

SCOTT: Huh ? Oh, this ... just someone who went missing.

JOEL: Your ex.

SCOTT: No. Someone very much present. I'll tell you who he is
           if you stay tonight.

14

5.   *Dazzling Summer sky, as clear as a favorite memory.*

JOEL: Memory of the cornflowers I grew back in the East
               and the sun in the blue deep sky.
               Bachelor buttons grew high,
               three foot stems. I'm lying on my back in the yard,
               the dusty day and the deep sky and the flowers waving
               blue on blue
               black and blue.

6. *Sudden night. Highway. A looming Drive-In Movie Theater screen.*

JOEL: The mountains are glowing there beyond the highway
               zoom
               in the dark / bruised blacknblue mountains
               zoom / woah ! What's this what's this jeezus what -
               Drivein ! Drivein ! Check it out ! Skyview Drivein!
               Huge slab o' gray light / right by the highway / big
                    bodies
               movin' around in the night - oh man ! Ain't that
                    something.
               Lookit that, between the black fields,
               the hills, giant ghost faces yeah ! And big ghost bodies,
                    whozit?
               Whozat? It's ... it's that ... that Frenchy guy / Belgian -
               y'know ... Van Damme - yeah. Van Damme, lit across
                    the night

               ... um... oh, what's this movie ... oh, it's, it's ...
               Timecop. Yeah. Usedta love movies, knew 'em all.
               When I was a kid, wished I could live in the movies ...
               loved the old Disney stuff / *Swiss Family Robinson* /
                    now how
               the hell did ostriches and tigers end up on a desert
                    island ? And
               the pirates / pirates / who was that that - pirate ...
               Burt Lancaster ! Yeah !
               That smile / smile woulda lit up the night.
               The Crimson Pirate / those striped tights / yeah /
                    funniest damn
               thing ... sexiest man I ever saw ... I wished I coulda
                    sailed
               away with the pirates / two hundred years ago / a
                    hundred
               years / a century sailing the deep black sea / the pirates
               and me / bandanas / cutlass / swoosh,

                                                               15

the creaking wood the wheel the stars flung across
the deep dark sky.

I call him my little pirate.
Darkeyes. Deep. Black as sky, black as night, my little
    pirate,
little sailor, let's get you a gold ring for your ear
then you will see in the dark.
You need to see in the dark.

7. *Houseboat.*

JOEL: I can handle my liquor, okay ? It's this goddamn
                 houseboat
             makin' me seasick.
             I have to go back to New York, *don't I ? Don't I ?*
             Gotta go back, back to ... sleet and rain in the winter,
             sweat and busted airconditioning in the summer.
             Back to the parking garage in the morning,
             the groceries at night, on the way home the drink,
             just a little one, that is - just one more -
             and then maybe a top-up and - what the hell,
             gimme the bottle.
             Weekend visits to visit Mom and Dad, flowers on
             their neat tiny graves, side by side under the pines
             the way they made me promise. Dad embalmed in
               whisky,
             Mom in Martini. An olive stuffed in her mouth.
             My bunches of limp calla lilies.
             Gotta goback.
             Staring out my office windows at the Chrysler building
             across the way, I imagine skysurfing down to land on
             a gargoyle, eaglehead, poised to fly away from
             here forever.

             Scott. Feeding and watering me. Monday drifts into
             Tuesday - days and nights softening, time runs like
             hot butter.
             Lying on his bed in the summer heat, he courts me,
             I always wanted to be courted,
             not just desired in dark corners after midnight.

SCOTT: Joel, stay with me.

JOEL: I can't. I have to go back to New York.
             There's a policy meeting on friday.

16

SCOTT: Policy *this*. So leave Thursday.

JOEL: I can't. I have to go home. I have to prepare.

SCOTT: Home ?

JOEL: They need me.

SCOTT: The hell they do.

JOEL: I take my job seriously.

SCOTT: And I take my *work* seriously.

JOEL: Work ? You roam around San Francisco housesitting
            houseboats - boatsitting ?

SCOTT: I'll have you know I am, in fact, a Republican's
            nightmare. I'm the demon king. That's my job ! I
            write poems and read a hell of a lot of books. And I
            know lots and lots of people who invite me to press
            junkets and then I write a cynical column about it
            and sell it to the *Bay Area Reporter* and everyone
            huffs and puffs when they read it but I *always spell
            their names right* so I get away with murder. And I
            publish my poems. Myself. Because no-one else's
            gonna do it for me.

JOEL: Are they good poems ?

SCOTT: Oh yes. And when I'm stuck, I steal from the best.

JOEL: Who's the best ?

SCOTT: Petronius. Sappho. Catullus.

JOEL: I feel kinda stupid suddenly. Is that allowed ?

SCOTT: Oh, bite me. C'mere.

JOEL: He touches my neck.
            The back of his hand brushes my wrist.

            Woah ! O God. I'm sorry Scott. I just had this ... flash ...
            that my Mom and Dad are gonna arrive home early
                and send you home with your tail between your
                legs and me to bed with no supper.

SCOTT: Aren't they in New York ?

JOEL: Just outside. Outside and underneath.

They're dead.

SCOTT: They don't sound dead.

JOEL: They have been known to line up at the foot of my
             bed,
             looking tragic and wounded. Not when I sleep alone,
             mind you.
             Only in company. Just when I'm about to ... when
             I'm ...

SCOTT: They can't get in here.

JOEL: Yeah right.

SCOTT: They can't. They're not welcome. I won't let 'em.
             They can't come in because I say so. Okay ?

JOEL: Okay ... so tell me about your boyfriend.

SCOTT: This ? This isn't my boyfriend.
             Okay. I'm seven years old.
             My Dad says 'I've something important to explain'.
             Everyone who is missing in Southeast Asia
             - prisoners of war -
             has their name stamped into a silver band.
             And the date they went missing.
             And we have to wear them to remember who's
             missing.
             Everyone gets a band. The woman in the store has one
             the man at the gas station has one
             all the kids in gradeschool have one. We are each
             given a band
             with a name and ...
             mine has a white star on a deep blue ground. See ?
             This means my Lieutenant Colonel was in the Air
             Force.
             And I prayed for him and I pray for him.

             I wear his band. Lieutenant Colonel James Young.
             Missing. July Six 1966.

             The North Vietnamese start releasing prisoners in
             seventythree - they all come home and they come
             through the airbase in my hometown and their
             pictures are on the tv news and in the papers.

             One girl, on the news.
             In a palegreen dress, kneehigh socks, Marcia Brady
             hair,
             running across the tarmac,

18

throwing herself on her dad ... 's nice, y'know ?
and I'm not sure if the man on my wrist is safe.
Or alive or dead.

And everyday the names of the homecoming prisoners
      are in the paper.
And who's died in captivity. And the unaccounted-for.
My pilot.
Lieutenant Colonel James Young.
Missing in action.
Unaccounted-for.
You ... have you ever been to the Vietnam memorial ?

JOEL: No, I haven't.

SCOTT: You should go.
          I went. To find his name.
          It isn't there.
          I wonder if he's home. Yet.

          I pray for him.
          In case nobody else does.
          I can't think of him behind bars, in a compound, in a
              jail,
          in a cage.

          I see him free, and happy,
          and in sunlight, and water,
          swimming, lungfulls of air and light.

          You ought to go to the memorial, Joel.

JOEL: Don't we deserve a monument ?

SCOTT: We who ?

JOEL: All of us who ... this disease ...

SCOTT: ...*this* disease ? Oh ... this disease. Mmm.
          I think we have to make our own memorials, Joel.
          Nobody's gonna do it for us.
          Kiss me.

JOEL: His hand tracing muscles I don't even know I have.
          He introduces me to my body for the first time.
          ... my jaw, the middle of my collarbone, pressing
              deeply
          into my calves, blood rushing into muscle fibre,
          my whole body suddenly shivering, letting go,
          I want someone to touch me I want someone to hold
              me I want to be safe

                                                          19

I want to sleep on my gentle lover's chest ...
his hand tracing waves and riptides and whirlpools
I'm drifting in the soft salt sea

I take in big deep lungfulls of him. I have to let go.
Let go.
He nuzzles my ear
I have to let go and lose ...lose ... control.
All the years of staying in control, staying in charge,
of keeping it all in.

The energy it takes to stay so angry
so tight
so ... frightened
Scott ... I'm scared -

He kisses my brow
and I'm no longer afraid of being frightened:
the beginning of courage.

The slow strong heartbeat, Joel and Scott,
we don't miss a beat.
On the soft cool bed, he turns off the lights.
A lapping of waves, the night and the city across the
    bay
and he opens all the windows, a curtain lifts in the
    breeze
he pulls my t shirt over my head
takes off my pants, undresses himself
kisses my shoulder
I'm scared. Of the feelings inside my feelings. Licks
    my chest -

SCOTT: Oh Joel, you taste of the sea.

JOEL: Yeah right. Mud and squid.

SCOTT: Joel, whatever are you so afraid of ?
             Oceans are made of 2 billion years of rain.

JOEL: Shapes, behind my eyes. The edges of the room alive,
                  rippling,
             my nerves squeezing outta my skin.

             The walls melt, drip and sway,
             the ocean bubbling in the bay ... clouds shifting,
             a rush of moonlight and a distant siren,
             and amazing in this heat
             a shower of soft rain,
             the curtain drifts in the breeze.
             What's this ? I never noticed this.

His earring, a tiny curl of gold.

SCOTT: It's so I can see at night.
            There's an acupuncture point for the eye right here.
            Sailors used to pierce their ears so they could see in the
                dark.

JOEL: ... Scott my pretty pirate, sailing the darkened seas
            two hundred years ago.
            I want to stay I want to play pirates.
            Guilt will take me back
            guilt will make me turn back East
            I want to stay and play with Scott, please,
            I want to stay.
            Don't make me come in yet.
            Just one more game, please.
            Don't make me go to sleep -

SCOTT: Joel... stay with me.

JOEL: I have to go.

SCOTT: You'll be back. I promise.
            One too many evenings smiling at the bagger at the
                checkout / unreturned smiles, hearing yourself 'how
                are you today ?' and realizing you don't care.
            Once too often paying top dollar in French restaurants
                for a platefull of sauce / and nights alone at home /
                eating
            Rice-a-Roni / the rain at the window / the nth rerun of
            Now Voyager on tv
            and you'll say fuck it.
            One thing will set you off, riding, one thing,
            but once you start you won't ever be able to stop
            you'll be on your way.

            Trust only movement.
            In movement there is blessing...

            You'll put it down to me of course. You will !
            You'll say: I'm moving out West to be with Scott !
            But it'll be you.
            Moving. Free. I'll pester you until you do.
            I won't quit. You have to come.

JOEL: Why me ?

SCOTT: Why not you ? I love you !

JOEL: What? First sight ?

SCOTT: Absolutely ! Love at first sight
            happens to everyone, all the time.
            Everyone's so scared by it, they don't follow through.
            They think it means giving everything up.
            Joel, I love you.

JOEL: No catch ? No conditions ?

SCOTT: Someone once was kind to me.
            I have to pass it on.
            You, too, have to pass it on.
            To whoever can hear.
            Let me tell you
            this: someone in
            some future time
            will think of us.

JOEL: He kisses my neck, down,
            my chest, down,
            my bellybutton and down,
            kisses it seems that nothing can ever erase.

8. *Manhattan. Summer dusk. Headlights streaming over freeways.*
    Joel in his apartment, alone. Staring at the neon and sundown.

JOEL: I had to go back to New York, didn't I ?
            I had to make my policy meeting. New York City -
            La Guardia airport a wet blur, August heat and hot
                rain.
            The freeways slithering around each other.
            Back in Manhattan I miss him within moments,
            city of cabs and sirens and steam rising from baked
                drains.
            A rainstorm roars like a tsunami down Lexington
                Avenue.

            I miss him. I miss him so much.

            In my apartment, the gleaming liquor bottles
            line up on the bar, half-full.
            One by one down the toilet.
            Proud and grateful. Scott, thank you I miss you thank
                you
            I want you I need to sleep on your chest feel the pulse
            in your neck sending me off, off ... to dream ... staring
            out my streaked apartment window,
            the first surge of knowing ...

22

knowing what ...?
A simple truth, simple as sun and ocean:
anything is possible.

'This is Scott. I can't take your call. Leave a message.
    Hi Joel.
I miss you. Wait for the beep ! Byeeeee!'

Scott ... uh ... Scott it's Joel.
Scott ? Please pick up. Scott ? Are you there ?
Pick. Up. The. Phone.
Where are you ? Okay, listen. At midnight tonight,
    your time,
go out on the deck
look at the water.
I'm going to push back the furniture here
and at the stroke of twelve I'm going to take your
    hand.
Close your eyes. You'll feel me. I promise.
And we are going to dance together. Okay ?
I'll see you at midnight.
And afterwards we'll sleep and dream together.
See you at twelve.

9. *Washington DC. Trees and green.*

JOEL: Zoom zoom. Freeway. First stop Washington DC.
               This is for you, Scott.
               Imagine a big black bird spreading wings, flightless,
                   dying,
               but for one brief moment before it dies
               it spreads enormous wide wings
               one last, vast stretch for the sky and the wind
               and the view over paradise.
               Now imagine this bird, its wings, transforming
               as the last breath leaves,
               transforms into something solid, black, obsidian ...
               hard black marble, a folded V, here in the green earth.
               And it's enormous, the size of a pteranodon ...
               and it's engraved with names. A myriad names.
               And they are dead people's names marked on the
                   wings of this black bird-god, this marble bird.
               And this is the Vietnam memorial.
               You don't come across it. Or find it
               - you come *into* it.
               It receives you,
               coaxes you in and builds ..

kinda builds with you.

And I wonder ... I wonder what kind of lord,
what kind of god presides over feelings like these ?
And I wonder I wonder how you cope with knowing
    you've
outlived your children ?
First it was Vietnam. Then it was our disease.
And it is a gay disease. It is it is of course it is ...
Well ...
isn't it ? ... I thought ... it was ... I usedta think
it was ... but ... now ... I don't know anymore ...
all I know is I would like to see the whole country
on its knees thanking us. Why aren't they all...
why isn't everyone offering flowers to a great stone
    monument, a great granite, volcanic monument like
    this why aren't they crying for us and our disease ?

A t-shirt slogan ...
I WANT A CURE AND I WANT MY FRIENDS BACK

neither of which is gonna happen.
So we're left with a quilt flapping in the rain.
And we're left with a chunk of black granite a
    grenade's throw from the White House.
And as you walk along this great wall of names, this
    big V,
a big black wingspan spread under the gray
    Washington sky,
sudden shafts of light through the clouds pierce and
pin the trees the lawns the monument.
The memorial. But it's more than a memorial because
    this is closer than memory this is present this is
    present moment
and you watch these people and you cannot / I cannot
be unmoved ... this black wall of the dead. Dead.
And this is what I see.
A couple in maybe their sixties walk up to the wall,
    he's in a sensible mac against the threat of rain his
    wife is grayhaired, groomed, in sensible shoes and
    they hold each other they hold. On. To. Each other.
    Looking. Searching. Looking. And I know what
    they're looking for they're looking for their son's
    name. No.

They're looking for their son.

And as they step forward and he holds her and they
    find it,
the single name / among so many names living names /
    they

start to tremble and they hold each other and
their boy went away and he's not coming home
and they hold onto each other
and it overtakes them they can't hold it back they've
    come to find their little boy
their little boy that they loved through fevers and
    measles
and first day at school
and first dates
and can I borrow the car Dad
and remembering Mother's Day with a late bunch of
    flowers
and they loved him
and they love him
and he's not coming home.
And he went away with all their prayers
and still he's not coming home and they wonder
why didn't he come home ? Did I pray wrong ? Why
    him ?
Didn't God hear ? He must have heard mustn't he ?
    He's God isn't he ? Did I pray wrong why didn't he
    hear me and send our son home safe and and
AND I WANT A CURE AND I WANT MY
    FRIENDS BACK AND WE THOUGHT WE'D
    LIVE TO BE OLD DIDN'T WE.

10. *Night highway. Freeway sounds. Rolling by, trucks lit like Xmas*
    trees.

JOEL: Men.
              First there was Christopher.
              His fingers gripped like a baby's, clutching me at
                  night, desperate.
              Decided he needed a wife and kids. As if they were
              accoutrements. Like a Filofax bound in Moroccan
                  leather.
              At the wedding reception, we all danced very gravely
                  to the
              Rolling Stones / You can't always get what you want /
                  Chris   took me into a corner. Whispered -
                  why do they always
              whisper ? - 'But the sex with you will always be the
                  best.'

              O I don't think so Christopher. Enjoy the suburbs.

              Then there was Sam.

He played the game didn't he?
Always boasting when he lived with me:
'Joel is everything I ever needed'
So why did you go Sam ?
Gone to play the game ?

All those young men on headspinning pillows /
    puppies
tired of the chase.
Young men, at parties, dancing with me
while their girlfriends pass out on vodka and gin.
They get married, they take out small ads
in the freebie gay papers:
'Straight-acting guy' 'Bi guy seeks sex buddy'
'Married but discreet.' Awww, discreet this !
'Non-scene, straight acting, no fems or fatties please.
    Your
photo ensures my reply'
Straight acting. How do you act straight ?
Bash fags ? Rape women ?
Invade small countries ?
Straightacting ...
Straitjacket
Men. I understand what you meant, Ma. I really do.
... 'men !'...
I wonder what they remember of me ?

Zoom. Freeway. *Zoom.*
Just outside Atlanta, Georgia. A hot, fragrant midnight.
Stop.

Here,
Under the taut freeways,
see ... over there. Men in packs,
waiting ...

eyes meet mine.
Men in black leather and biker boots,
fake cops, mustachioed, bulging.
Pierced tits -

'Hey now, these ain't tits, they're pecs' -
honey, when you're sellin' 'em, they're tits.
Let's talk, boys. You big butch things.
What shall we discuss ?
Football, rockclimbing,
hammering nails with the flat of your hand ?

Nope. These boys want to talk about fabrics and
    furnishings.
Drapes that match the cat.

Share recipes for calamari in ginger sauce.
Yep. The bigger they are, the nellier they are.
Men touching me as I pass among them.

Men sucking face. Shifty eyes. Men, aloof.

Oh guys the game's up. What's the point guys ?

HEY GUYS, WHAT'S THE POINT ?
Oops. That was really loud ... suddenly
a woman approaches me. In a black satin kaftan
Billowing.

MA: I don't think they heard that in Illinois honey.
   You from outta town ?

JOEL: I'm driving to San Francisco.

MA: Well didja get lost hon ? It's THAT WAY.

JOEL: I've been driving a long time.
   I'm gonna surprise my honey.

MA: He'll get an even bigger surprise if you don't wear one
   o'these.

JOEL: What are you, the morality police ?

MA: Honey, bite me. I'm Ma Deva of the latex.

JOEL: Sor-*reee*.
   Doesn't Jessye Norman want her dress back ?

MA: Oh, you're from New York.

JOEL: Just what are you doing here. Exactly ?

MA: Honey, this disease has got to go. Enough.
   I hand out the condoms. Cumcatchers.
   Baby - do you smoke ?

JOEL: No.

MA: I don't mean tobacco.

JOEL: Oh. No. Not any more.

MA: Really ? I'm just an old dope diva at heart. Ahhhh ...
   phhtttt ... anyway ... this disease has got to go.
   So here I am on condom patrol. Phhhttt. Tuesdays and
    Thursdays I do meal deliveries for Project Angel

Food, next month I'll be shimmyin' my saggy ass
through midtown Atlanta for the AIDS walk, see
you in Piedmont Park maybe, hon ? Bring your
friend. Then - God knows why GOD knows why -
I'm gettin' 'em all organized for a bike-a-thon so
I'll be pedallin' this sorry ass all over Interstate
Seventy-Five ... a gal's gotta do somethin', babe,
right ? Know what I'm sayin', sugar ? Phhhttt. Do
ya think this stuff is any good for ya ?

JOEL: Whatever works.

MA: My sentiments EXACTLY !
             You'd've liked my Danny. My darling Danny, died
                 last month.
JOEL: Danny.

MA: Danny. Danny boy. 'O Danny boy, the lights / the
                 lights are callin'' - my boy. Babe, lemme tell ya,
                 when your one-and-only baby dies, a girl has gotta
                 do SOMETHING. Hell.
             Who wants to outlive their kids ?
             ... awww, nuts. So here I is. Passin' out the plastic -
                 my, there's a lotta boys here tonight. I hope I
                 brought enough with me ... such nice boys. I often
                 wonder which of them - if any - knew Danny. You
                 know what I mean, kid. Knew him.
             O well. No point bein' polite. No point in standing on
                 ceremony.
             Okay boys, let's wrap it in plastic !
             He left me these.

JOEL: (She shakes her hair and there on her ears
             a pair of lovely earrings,
             dangling big and brassy, just like her.)

MA: Like 'em ? My legacy. He said I could choose anything
                 I liked.
             I chose these. Now why, I asked, why do you have a
                 pair of faux diamond earrings in your jewelry case?
                 He said they were his grandmother's. *Please.*
             His grandmother would not have been caught *dead* in
                 these.
             You know the truth. Danny boy wore these damn
                 danglers ev'ry Saturday night. He loved to play
                 dress up.
             He shoulda gone into the musical theatre.
             Whaddya think ? Anyways ... the day he dies, I get the
                 call from his lover, Lawrence. Who is a doctor,
                 which was what I always wanted, a doctor in the

28

family, Lawrence, a nice boy, a nice Jewish boy,
Lawrence said I was born into the wrong faith,
I said honey, I was a Jewish Momma in my last
lifetime, this time round I'm a dope-smokin' pagan!
Hah !

Lawrence says come quick, get to the hospital, it's
only a matter of time - I said honey, quelle surprise,
Danny's been hanging on with white knuckles for
months, I mean *let go*. Kid, what is it that keeps us
all hangin' on in there ?

What is it, kid ? Can you tell me ?

I think: I'll wear these special earrings to say g'bye to
Danny so I pull a brush thru my hair and give
myself two big lipfulls of Viva Glam so's I can
give him a kiss that'll see him into the   next
world. I mean a kiss that an autopsy can't shift and
I grab my earrings and hell, I'm still fastening them
while I'm running for the elevator and I get there
and ...

oh, he looks beautiful. Really beautiful. And I kiss him
on the cheek. Big red Viva Glam imprint right here
- and he looks at me all teary and of course he
cannot speak by this point and so all you can do is
gaze at him. And oh Lord he's *ready, he's ready to
go*, oh God he's wanted to go for weeks. I was even
toying with calling that Dr Kevorkian fella. Oh
dear. And he's trying to say something and I press
my finger to his lips, oh, a tender moment. A very
touching gesture, I thought. I say baby, don't try
and say anything, look, look and toss my head so he
can see the earrings and I say aren't they beautiful,
I'll treasure them forever and thank you and thank
you - he tries to ... uh uh uh ... gasp a word ... no
use. Lawrence is crumpled in a corner, beside
himself, I say Lawrence, move your ass over here
and hold this boy. I say to Danny, let go, I say let
go, don't hang around on our account, Momma's
here, I love you, Lawrence is here, he loves you,
c'mon baby, let go, like in that movie *Bedside
Companion* -

JOEL: *Longtime Companion*

MA: - Huh? Whatever you say. And he goes. Moves on.
Just slips away. And Lawrence and me hug each
other and weep and thank god he's in a better place
now. And we go home. Except that I stop off at
every bar I can think of on the way home.

For my own little private wake. And eventually I get
home. I get to my bedroom and I undress and I'm
starting to cry and I sit at my make-up table, in

front of my mirror, like Carroll Baker in *The Carpetbaggers*, God, Danny loved that movie, and the mascara is running down and the Viva Glam is all smeary, I look like a ... one of those French torch singers. After a real fruity rendition of *Je Ne Regrette Rien*. And I look at myself. I shake my hair. And I see I'm wearing odd earrings. I'd grabbed odd earrings in my rush to the hospital. Well, Danny had noticed. He'd been trying to tell me. He'd been trying to say 'You dumb broad ! What the fuck have you got on your ears!' That boy of mine, he always had such good taste. I'll be a schlep forever. He took years off me. Well, guess I got 'em all back now.

I guess that's the deal. He was a research chemist. Clever boy.

I was so proud of him. I never let a day go by, I didn't tell him how proud of him I was. I think it's real important to do that. Can you believe it ? Think of all the cures and vaccines and powders and potions that will never be discovered now that my Danny won't be around to do it.

All the good taste has gone from America.
It died in the 'nineties.

JOEL: We never had any.

MA: Hmm. Well there's no hope now babe. So.
Where'd ya say you were headed ?

JOEL: A little place near San Francisco. Called Sausalito.
I'm going to see my honey ... I'm going to find the Pacific.

MA: Well good for yew ! Go for it hon.
You two take care of each other.
And remember - you wrap it in plastic !
And do me one other favor ... when you get there ... keep on goin'.

JOEL: Mmm ?

MA: When ya get to the edge of the continent, keep goin'.
Keep headin' west.
Oh honey, it doesn't all begin and end with America.

JOEL: Thanks. For what you're doing.

MA: Aw, hon. Enlightened self-interest. I mean, I'd go crazy ... what's a mother to do ?

11.   *Texas. Shimmering heat & light.*
              Joel, leaning against his car, gulping bottled water.

JOEL: Texas. Yee-ha ! Vast and flat / clouds bigger than the
                 sky.
              My brother-in-law came from Texas. His dad killed
                 himself.
              Flew his private plane in a straight line / down /
                 vertical
              smashed into the driedup levee.
              Now why would he do that ?
              Because he was going broke.
              So his wife could collect the insurance.
              I guess a man who can't provide for his family ain't no
                 man at all.
              I guess a man who cracks in the middle / making ends
                 meet,
              I guess a man like that won't have no wife of his get
                 no job
              and why would she want to anyway?
              A man like that don't deserve no wife.
              Or kids who need a dad.

12. *Arizona. Late afternoon.*

JOEL: Arizona desert -
              endless highway -
              big sky, like in *Zabriskie Point.*

              Suddenly a gas station and a 1960's diner -
              like a dinosaur bird, trapped.

              A bone-white 'V' in the middle of the desert.

              These places grew up outta the sand
              these places are like clumps o'cactus.
              A hunnerd years old and suckin up rain an' tears from
                 the sand
              these places.
              Red neon.
              Open.
              Open.
              Open.
              Waitresses with huge hair and name tags
              here's Carmen slinging a jug o'ice tea
              there's Juanita with a stack o'pancakes,

armfuls of syrup and whipped butter.
Women who came from the East and couldn't go no
    further, women who just stopped
and gave up the trek, right here.
Women in Buicks and old Studebakers
women whose cars ran outta gas same time as
their purses ran outta bills / whose men ran out.
They stick together, these women in desert diners and
    highway truck stops.
Grownup girl scouts in the desert.
All growed up selling melted cookies.

Worlds rushin' by these diners.
Women who sank to their knees, exhausted
and waited for someone to wrap a diner around them.
And they stayed and they stay.

13. Diner. Big windows.

JOEL: And I'm sitting at the counter, eating, thinking this an'
                 that and there's a woman sitting next to me, another
                 customer, in a floppy hat and a cotton jacket and
                 cotton khaki shorts, a woman who looks like she's
                 about sixty but she's kinda lean and healthy and it's
                 really hard to tell. She turns and smiles at me and
                 it's all there in her eyes. Completely open, big
                 darkbrown sad sad eyes, shining, as if she's always
                 lived on the edge of tears, but she might be really
                 really happy to the point of ... she looks kinda ...
                 ecstatic. Ec - static.

                 Hi.

MYRA: Hello.
                 Isn't it lovely ?

JOEL: Excuse me?

MYRA: This place. It has ... Nineteen Sixty-Seven written all
                 over it, don't you think. Ugly thing.

JOEL: What was it with the sixties ?
                 Mr Tambourine Man ? Granny glasses ?

MYRA: We were all so ... so busy running around we ... some
                 bad taste got by unnoticed -

32

JOEL:	Some ?
MYRA:	A lot. We all thought ... thought it was going to change -
JOEL:	What was ?
MYRA:	Human nature, I think. Yes. The nature of the beast.
JOEL:	I'd say you were mistaken.
MYRA:	Would you ? We had a sense of possibilities. That's why the Republicans keep trashing the sixties. *Forrest Gump* indeed! Did you see that movie ? Reactionary ka-ka, excuse my French. We simply failed to take into account that there was money to be made. Is there always money to be made do you think ? Are you in a hurry ?
JOEL:	More or less. OK. Today, I'm in less of a hurry.
MYRA:	Oh, good. May I buy you your lunch ?
JOEL:	Are you a serial killer ?
MYRA:	Oh, no. no, not at all.
JOEL:	Okay then, yes ! I love this about this country. Us. We make friends easily. Don't we. Don't you think ? Don't we ? My name is Joel.
MYRA:	Hello Joel. I'm Myra.
JOEL:	Are you lonely here ?
MYRA:	A little. You understand this of course.
JOEL:	Yes. Is it obvious ?
MYRA:	Most things are obvious aren't they ? If we just stop ... chattering.
JOEL:	Do you live alone?.
MYRA:	Are *you* a serial killer? I live with a cat. I know, I know, a single lady and a cat.
JOEL:	Is it a nice cat?

MYRA: Oh yes. She never seems to mind what mood I'm in.

JOEL: Cuddles without conditions.

MYRA: Something like that. My husband didn't understand
           this ...
           Most men don't ...
           Can you tell me why this is ? ... Most men don't
               understand cuddle and touch without sex being
               involved.
           I wanted to be held and he took it as a need ... a
               prelude ... to sex. What is that about ?

JOEL: Maybe he was ... afraid ?

MYRA: Afraid of a kiss ???

JOEL: Terrified.

MYRA: Terrified ? I'm not so sure.

JOEL: Maybe just confused...

MYRA: In what way ?

JOEL: Well, you know ... your ... the genitals get confused
           with the ... with ...

MYRA: Your heart.

JOEL: Yes. Your heart. Straight men, gay men ... I usedta
               think gay men especially, now I'm sure it's men
               men. So, uh, Myra, what do you do ? For money ?
               Work ? Stuff ?

MYRA: Teach. Second grade.

JOEL: Ah. Good age ... do you have any family ?

MYRA: Not now. My daughter died.

JOEL: Ah. Hmmm. I'm sorry. How'd she -

MYRA: She killed herself.

JOEL: I'm sorry. young ?

MYRA: Twenty.

JOEL: Oh. Oh. I'm sorry. Umm ... recent ?

34

MYRA:	Five years.
JOEL:	Are you okay with it ?
MYRA:	Okay ?
JOEL:	I mean ... how are you handling ? Now ?
MYRA:	She's certainly ... certainly the central presence in my life
JOEL:	How did she....?
MYRA:	Die ? She o/d'd. She was a junkie. I didn't know. The thing is ... isn't it odd ? The way we compartmentalize our lives ? We found her journals and it was like reading ... it was reading ... the thoughts of a person that I had never met ... someone I never knew. Completely hidden from us.
JOEL:	Us?
MYRA:	Her father. Me. Us. She wore ... a mask ? No. An *identity* for us. She ... dissembled ? No. Too harsh. She presented a face to us. I had no idea what else was going on. The pain she was in. That is the hardest, to read that pain and not to have ... we weren't there for her. I trust that she knows how much we love her. Are you going to eat your pickle ?
JOEL:	Ah, no, please. My parents were buried with a bottle. Each.
MYRA:	I don't drink. Not now. It seems ... rude. I don't want to risk ... missing anything. I need to feel the grief. Not drown it. In case she's trying to tell me something. What pain could have been so terrible ?
JOEL:	She didn't say ?
MYRA:	Not yet. I'm trying to understand. And I want to understand ... the world that claimed her.
JOEL:	Maybe she's your guardian angel.
MYRA:	Do you think so ? That would be nice, wouldn't it ? That would be lovely.

JOEL: What does your husband feel about it ?

MYRA: Oh. Oh no. We're separated. I got the cat.
               When .. um ... when a child dies, most marriages ...
               few marriages survive this.

JOEL: She watches me eat. In silence. The sun is low. Dark
                    coffee
               in the soft warm stillness. Her face is quiet.
               All cried out, five years of crying.
               She takes the bill from the waitress.

               Thank you. For lunch.

MYRA: Drive safely. Give my love to wherever you're going.

14. Sierra Nevada. Morning. Dusty, magic light.

JOEL: Swing across the Nevada State Line
               into California -
               the cattle make me feel welcome.

               What's this ?

               There in the shadow-and-butter barnyard light are two
                    beasts,
               big one on top,
               banging away. A bull, a long-suffering cow ?
               NO! A TRIUMPH ! NOW I'VE SEEN
                    EVERYTHING !
               Two sets of udders sloshing away !
               Lesbian cows !

               LESBIAN COWS GREET YOU AT
               THE BORDER OF NEVADA !
               Here in the shadow of the Sierra Nevada. Yesssss!
               Scientific proof ! It's COMPLETELY NATURAL !

               Girl cattle and girl catttle at it !
               Boy snakes curling around boy snakes !
               Little girl skunks
               squirting lovely stink over little girlfriend skunks.
                    Yesssss!
               From Gardnerville Nevada to Coyote Arizona to
               Desert Rock California,
               it's a queer old world.

36

15. *Desert Rock, California. Starlite motel. Neon. Through the window, last sunset glow.*

JOEL: Desert Rock, California. Starlite Motel. Oh my.
'Swimming pool and jacuzzi / icemaker on every floor
/ the comfort of centralized air conditioning'

Is this the Elvis suite ?
Leopardprint nagahide headboard.
Very tasteful.
Oh Ma, you'd be in heaven. Hey Ma, is your heaven
    all nagahide and padded plastic cocktail bars ?
A big pink mirror behind the bar, engraved with pink
    elephants, little smiley elephants, champagne
    glasses held high in their little trunks ?

Wow. What a view. Empty Mojave Desert. Purple sky.
B movie country. There oughta be some giant mutant
    ants prowling out there, Leo G Carroll chased down
    by a big ole overgrown tarantula.

Midnight at the oasis.
Cable tv in ev'ry room. I love America. Okay. Let'
    see. What's the game plan ? We'll grab a shower,
    order in some food.
I guess they have room service ? Order in some sushi,
    a little filet mignon. Yeah right. In this place ?
    Fatburger and fries. Let's see here.

Click.

American Movie Classics. Ogod. Mickey Rooney and
    Judy. The amphetamine twins !
HEY GANG, LET'S PUT ON A SHOW !
Click.
HBO.
Liza ! With a z! *Pookie !* Ogod it's the queen's own
    channel ! Liza honey ! Mama ... Mama... can you
    hear me Mama ... it's Liza, Mama ... this song's for
    you ! Liza, Liza ... stop blinking, Liza ... O Liza
    honey, the *hair !*
I love women who found a style in nineteen seveny-
    two and just ... *stuck with it.* Life may be a cabaret
    old chum
but some of us changed our hairstyle from time to
    time ...
Liza. Honey. Mama's dead.
She's *dead,* hear me girl ? Move on ! Click.

Bette Davis ! Gee, Desert Rock is Fag Central after all!

DON'T LET'S ASK FOR THE MOON,
WE HAVE THE STARS.

Click. We have the stars.

Scifichannel Weatherchannel Learning channel History
    channel channelchannel.
Romance channel. Gossip channel. Family Values
    channel.
Sex and Violence channel. Jesus channel.
What's it all for channel, where am I going channel.
He loves me he loves me not channel.
I hope I'm doing the right thing channel.
Missing in action channel.
There's got to be more than this channel.
Fucked if I know what it is channel.
But I'll die trying to find out channel. Click.

Infomercials. I love them ... I need one of those ...
Soloflexbowflexabdominizerthighmaster
nordictracknordicflex
cockflexmindflexbrainbuster click.

Omigod. Dionne Warwick's Psychic Friends Network.
$3.95 A MINUTE ! Go girl go ! Walk on by baby !
    Yeah !
Coin it in girl !
Click. Woah ! Desert Rock's own porno channel !
Escort services. Massage service ...
'I'm Misty, try me !' I don't think so, darlin'.
Oh.
'I'm Gennifer and I'm waiting for your call !'
She's working her way thru college. Atta girl.
Oh. Oh.
Oh. Call 1-900-PISS ...
... call me old-fashioned ...
Oh. My. Great ! Snippets from the porno movie
    selections !
O great ... I love the music ... the music's always the
    same
... good for them. How come that never happens
when I order a pizza ?

I could call in a cowboy. Couldn't I ?
1-900-RAWHIDE !

Oh.
Oh.

'For men with special tastes -'
that's me ! -

' - women with cocks !'
Goodness.
Women with cocks.
Yeah right. Okay, okay, I get it -
I'm straight. Really !
I just like my girlfriend to have a cock.
Well it's all happening here in Desert Rock.
Where's the Christian channel ?

Click.

Aerobics for Jesus.
The lycra of Turin !
Oh dear.
She doesn't look very *redeemed*.
Click. And off. Click.

16. *California hills. Night.*

JOEL: Here in the dark hills the road rears and bucks and
                  terrifies.

               I'm dreaming of safety,
               of holding you tonight in a safe place.
               A net of light spreads across the plain.
               Civilization at last ! San Jose !

               'LA is a great big freeway / put a hundred down and
                  buy a car'
               Thank the suburbs for being there,
               now ride over them on the taut freeways -

               my face in the rearview mirror
               great. See these lines ? They're mine.
               I earned them.
               See these creases ?
               They're all mine. I lived 'em, every one.

17. *Santa Carla. Gas Station.*

JOEL: Santa Carla.
          Stop for gas. Little gas station, busy little downtown,
          a major intersection, the converging streets are
                  jammed.

Horns honking, white boys with
buzzcuts driving shiny white trucks and expensive
    Jeeps,
Mexican families staring through muddy windshields;
    staring down at the blacktop, or off into a hazy
    distance.

The gas station, the intersection, the downtown,
    overlooked
by high green hills that burst out of the streets
    themselves.
Thick dust and a sun clamped to the sky.

I buy a Snickers bar from the old grizzled guy at the
gas station. He looks bored. So he should. I'd be
    witless,
working here in the middle of this turnpike ...

I ask the quickest way to Sausalito. He waves a hand,
    towards a South-pointing avenue.

Is it far ? No. Not far. Nearly there. Nearly there.
    Scott -

I clamber into the car.

18. *Manhattan. Joel's empty apartment.*

JOEL: This is Joel. Sorry, can't take your call right now !
                Name rank and serial number please and I'll get back
                    to you ASAP !
                Here comes the beep ... *beeeep !*

SCOTT: Joel, Joel ... hey ... it's me it's Scott ... pick up ... hey
                    ...
                are you screening your calls ? ...
                Joel ...
                this is Scott ... hey Joel ... I guess you're out. Okay.
                Listen.
                I'll take you to a special location. It won't take long. In
                    fact you may be there already.
                It may take you a while to get your head around that
                    one !
                A long bumpy road but always the end in sight, a light
                    over the next hill, round the next bend, at the edge
                    of town,
                in the sky beyond the city limit. It's there and then it's
                    here, and it's not what we were looking for.

Not at all.
Be careful what you pray for. You just might get it.
 We long for a home - a house and a yard and a dog
 but suddenly it's
not what we thought we needed.
There's a little song about that. And you may say to
 yourself ... this is not
my ... beautiful house ...
there are little songs about everything.

So get moving Joel. This is Scott telling you to get
moving

only movement
trust only movement, Joel.
So have a pee before you leave and don't even think
 about stopping til you need to fill up on gas.
And all the stars who ever were are parking cars
and pumping gas -
See ? Little songs about everything.

Now get moving.

See ya.

19. Sausalito. Traffic jam.

JOEL: The worst feeling on the road is when you're two
 blocks away and you can see the place you need to
 be and there's suddenly the King Kong of traffic
 jams, red flares burning across three lanes of
 freeway and emergency trucks and firemen -cute
 firemen - and paramedics
and efficient dykes driving ambulances, women you'd
 trust your life to -
Stuck here with his place in sight and
an ocean to go splash in together.
God I hope he's in what if he's not in
I should have phoned. Oh he'll be in.
Let him be in.

Here we go. Now we're movin'.
Road along the waterfront
the village
the restaurants
the boys and girls out in the evening
the gorgeous houses stacked up on the hill.

When Scott'n me have finished travelling and moving
    around,
we'll come back and settle in a house up on the hill, up
    there,
up above the houseboats
swaying in the wind and earthquakes,
storms and weather / Joel and Scott
the folks who live on the hill.
We're here. This is it -

The boats clamped together,
old hippie houseboats and chichi houseboats side by
    side.
The tide racing in the bay.
San Francisco water meeting San Pablo water.
I'm coming for ya Scott you were right you were right
it doesn't take anything to get on the road.

Scott, this really is an old hippie hideaway.

20. *Houseboat. Afternoon light filters through drifting curtains.*

JOEL: Incense and mandalas and photos of dead gurus
               stapled to the walls.
               I don't remember this.
               Driftwood and old seashells.
               Where the hell is Scott ?

               Please Scott, tell me you haven't moved.
               Scott you would have told me wouldn't you
               tell me you haven't moved on.

               Where is he ?
               Where is anyone ...
               Scott !
               Scott !

               Oh. Oh hi.

               In Madras cotton and crumpled velvet,
               she looks like a delinquent heron that hasn't eaten for
                   days.
               A rage of hair;
               Bette Davis in *All About Eve*.
               Her lip is pierced, her brow is pierced,
               a dozen rings clamped through her left ear.
               She has a tattoo of a lizard on her neck, right here ...

42

She has Scott's eyes.
His sister ?
She's wonderful.

JOEL: Hi. Who are you ?

DHARMA: I live here.
             Who are you ?

JOEL: Joel.

DHARMA: I'm sorry, but ... this is ... like, private.

JOEL: I'm Scott's friend. Joel.

DHARMA: Ummmm Scott. Oh okokok. Cool.

JOEL: I just drove from New York City.

DHARMA: O wow. Was it far ?

JOEL: It took me five days.

DHARMA: Intense. Nonstop huh ? Cool. Wow.

JOEL: Are you his sister ?

DHARMA: Umno. It's my place. Do you have any weed ?

JOEL: No.

DHARMA: Right on. Drugs are a bad scene, man.
             Um. Do you have any acid ?

JOEL: No.

DHARMA: I drop some acid, like, once a week. Keeps me
                 spiritually toned.

JOEL: I stayed here a few days. With Scott. It's nice.
             You rent it ?

DHARMA: Ummno. It's my Dad's place. My Dad's kinda ...
                 what's the word ... rich. But - no - no - it's cool ...
                 he's working on it.
             He's ... like spiritually ... *trying,* y' know. Like, he
                 donates money. To charity. Can I make you some
                 tea ? I have ginseng. It'll detoxify you. After your
                 trip. O man, you drove across America ? I couldn't
                 handle it, oh, America, it's so ... so ... um ... *what's
                 the word ... fucked* ... yeah ? The Midwest, man,

43

ugh. So material. And they eat white bread *all the time* and they build houses next to nuclear waste dumps and have all these mutant babies. The United States, I just can't handle it.

JOEL: Are you from San Francisco ?

DHARMA: Umno.
I'm from Topeka ... Kansas.

JOEL: Ah. Are you at school ?

DHARMA: No. Well ... huh ... university of life, man. Y'know.

JOEL: Right, right ... so ... what does your Dad do ?

DHARMA: Um ... he builds real estate. But it's okay. It is. It is. It's cool. Guru Ma, that's my guru, she says the world will end in 1999. We're gonna be hit by a ... a ... um ... giant meteorite. And there'll be a 20000 foot tidal wave and California will be ... will be ...

JOEL: Wet.

DHARMA: Yeah.

JOEL: A houseboat will come in handy, then.

DHARMA: Hmm ? Oh ... humor ... cool. No, see, no. I'm moving to Montana. That's the only place that's gonna be saved. I'm leaving for my Dad's ranch as soon as I complete my karmic mission in the Bay Area.

JOEL: That's a really nice tattoo.

DHARMA: Yeah ? Thanks ... Lizard King, man.
Jim Morrison told me to do it.
Guru Ma channels Jim Morrison.
You should come to one of our meetings.
Jim isn't dead. He faked it.
He's in Tibet studying with the Mahatmas ... what ?

JOEL: I'm sorry ... do you ever get spinach caught in your lipring ?

DHARMA: I don't eat.
I live on prana.
Do you want icecream ? I have ginseng icecream.
It doesn't count. It's a spiritual food.
Do you want tea ? Did I ask you that ?

JOEL: No thanks. I just need to know when Scott's coming
             home -

DHARMA: Scott ... ummm Scott is a way cool spirit.
             Goodvibe guy.
             He was housesitting for a while.

JOEL: Yes. I know. Oh. I missed him.
             I shoulda called. I'm crap at surprising people.

DHARMA: Yeah. He's moved on.
             He might check in later tonight.

JOEL: Well, um, I could ... call or ... maybe I should -

DHARMA: - you should have some tea.

JOEL: I should find a motel. Well. Ok. I'll have to ...
             do you have a new address ? For Scott ? Or a number ?

DHARMA: Scott hates spinach.

JOEL: What ?

DHARMA: My lipring ? Spinach ? Scott. Scott turned me on to
             piercing.

JOEL: So you can see in the dark !

DHARMA: No ... I pierce to ... to ... remember. Each one of these
             is for
             a friend of mine who died with AIDS.
             This is Caleb
             this is Alex
             this is Josh
             this is Naomi
             this is Andrew
             this is Marco
             and this is for my friend Nilu ... she was so wonderful
             and this ...
             and this is...
             this is Scott.

JOEL: What ?

DHARMA: Yeah. It's new. It still hurts.

JOEL: Scott ...
             he ... moved on ?

DHARMA: Yeah. His next incarnation will probably be as

a fourth plane master. He was very ... uh ... *is* ... is very spiritual.

JOEL: Spiritual.

DHARMA: Yeah. If you talk to him, like tonight, you know, tell him
Dharma says ... hey.
Listen, I gotta kick you out now. I still have to meditate.
And cook up some rice for the potluck tonight.

JOEL: Dharma ... tell me your name.

DHARMA: Dharma.

JOEL: Tell me your .... your birth name.
What does your Dad call you ? Please.
I really need to know. Please.

DHARMA: Um. OK. Um ... it's ... Deirdre.

JOEL: Deirdre.
That's a beautiful name.
I hope you ... grow back into it.
I'll ... I'm gonna ... go now ... I'll ... get outta your hair...

DHARMA: Oh. Yeah. Ok. Nice meeting you Joel.
Joel. *Joel.* Oh ! Joel !
Scott left something for you !
Oh wow. I nearly forgot. Wow. *Bad* karma man.

JOEL: She fetches a little brown parcel. Written on the package -
'To Joel.
With all my heart
your fellow traveller,
Scott'

JOEL: Deirdre ? Where'd his body go ?

DHARMA: Back.

JOEL: Back ?

DHARMA: Where it came from.

JOEL: You see I ... I don't even know where he was from. I always thought his accent was ... from the East Coast ... was kinda Pittsburgh.

DHARMA: No man, hee hee, o man ... that's so *sweet* ...
             Pittsburgh.
             No ... back. Where he came from.
             The ocean.
             We burned him, we took the ash to the ocean.
             Fire and water. Cool, huh ? Scott was, like, *really*
             pleased.

JOEL: Deirdre ? Where ?
             What beach ?

DHARMA: Okay ... South on Highway One. About two hours. By
             Lighthouse Point. You can't miss it. You'll feel it.
             Pittsburgh ? That's so funny. That's so sweet ... no. He
             only ever went East once in his whole life, to
             Washington DC.
             Had to see the Vietnam Memorial. War, man. Bad
             scene.
             I couldn't handle it.
             No. He wasn't from Pennsylvania.
             He was from right here in California.
             Little place out in the Mojave. South of Baker,
             East of Barstow. Little place called Desert Rock.

JOEL: Deirdre ... Dharma. Thanks. You're ... cool.

DHARMA: Yeah ? Well. You know you gotta stay cool, right ?
             Else, we'd spend our whole lives crying, huh ?

JOEL: Dharma, hey, whatever works.

DHARMA: Yeah man. Whatever helps get us through it.

21. Beach. Radiant Sundown.

JOEL: Around six-fifteen / in the evening
             the sky turns vast lilac and green
             and the mountains turn purple, indigo
             and then some colors I never saw before
             and some colors I never heard of
             and the highway goes on forever.

             A beach. Honey-colored sand. The sun slides into the
             ocean.
             Wide low breakers, pink surf.
             Last shafts of light falling to the ocean floor
             through wave and riptide and whirlpool.

I open his gift,
pocket the wrapping.
I'm not leaving any more messes behind me.

A silver band.

Lieutenant Colonel James Young.
Missing in action. Uunaccounted-for.
Scott.
I don't mind if it was your time to move on.
I mind that you never got to hear me say
Scott, I love you.

I want a cure and I want my friends back
so they can hear me say I love you.

Scott, I need to know I'm not alone on this long road.

Trust only movement ?
Only movement ?
Okay, Scott.
Okay. C'mon.
C'mon Scott.
Dance with me.
Dance.

Oh, Scott, I love you.

We've such a long drive ahead of us.